how2become

RAPID STUDY SKILLS FOR STUDENTS: ACE YOUR TIME MANAGEMENT POCKETBOOK

www.How2Become.com

Orders: Please contact How2Become Ltd, Suite 3, 40 Churchill Square Business Centre, Kings Hill, Kent ME19 4YU.

You can order through Amazon.co.uk under ISBN 9781912370467, via the website www.How2Become.com, Gardners or Bertrams.

ISBN: 9781912370467

First published in 2018 by How2Become Ltd.

Typeset for How2Become Ltd by Jacob Senior.

Disclaimer

Every effort has been made to ensure that the information contained within this guide is accurate at the time of publication. How2Become Ltd is not responsible for anyone failing any part of any selection process as a result of the information contained within this guide. How2Become Ltd and their authors cannot accept any responsibility for any errors or omissions within this guide, however caused. No responsibility for loss or damage occasioned by any person acting, or refraining from action, as a result of the material in this publication can be accepted by How2Become Ltd.

The information within this guide does not represent the views of any third party service or organisation.

CONTENTS

INTRODUCTION

Welcome to your guide, *Ace Your Time Management*. In this book, you'll learn everything you need in order to be as efficient as possible with your time management. We'll provide you with tips, advice, exercises, and explanations in order to put you in the best position to manage your time.

Whether you're a student at school or university, or an employee in the workplace, time management is absolutely essential. No matter how skilled you are in your studies, improper use of your time will result in a rush to meet deadlines. In turn, this will cause your work to be of a lower quality, and raise your stress levels – making your studies much less enjoyable. So, it definitely pays to find ways of managing your time effectively, so that you can be at peak performance.

In this book, we'll be covering the main areas of time management that students will find useful:

1.   An introduction to what time management is, and why it's beneficial.

2.   A guide to improving your time management skills both in an exam and generally during your studies.

3.   How to identify where you're losing time, and how you can reclaim it!

4.   A guide to getting the most out of your studies.

To begin, let's get started with the basics: what time management is, when exactly you'll need it, and how to begin your journey to managing your time better!

WHAT IS TIME MANAGEMENT?

A sad fact about life is that we all have limited time. It often seems as though there aren't enough hours in a day; we might have a lot of plans about what to do from day to day, but it's hard to juggle between the things we *want* to do and the things we *need* to do.

As a student, this is particularly difficult because there's so much going on at both school and university. Between your studies, personal life, and taking care of yourself, it can be hard to balance all of your everyday duties as a student. Many students struggle to maintain a balance between all of their activities, meaning that their social life or studies suffer as a result of poor time management. If this rings true for you, then you definitely stand to benefit from learning time management techniques.

What is Time Management?

Time management is the art of making the most of the time you have, to get as much done as possible. This sounds straightforward enough, but many people struggle to manage their time effectively. To make time management easier to understand, let's divide it into the following categories:

- Devoting the perfect amount of time to each of your tasks, to ensure that the quality of your work is even throughout;

- Time-keeping skills to keep track of how long you have left to complete a task;

- Finding ways to maximise your efficiency during your working hours so that you have more time to spend on other activities;

- Knowing when to stop working to avoid diminishing returns in your work.

This book will examine these four major skills, as well as ways for you to improve them.

Where and When is Time Management Important?

Time management is an important skill across all subjects and academic disciplines. As a student, you need to be able to effectively use your time in the following environments:

1. When reading material or completing homework for weekly or fortnightly assessments.

2. When completing coursework such as essays, dissertations, and other projects.

3. When planning lab-work and other projects which involve more logistics than your average essay.

4. When preparing and revising for your exams.

5. When you're actually sitting an exam, and need to manage your time to ensure

that you complete the entire test to the best of your ability.

No matter what subject (or subjects) you're taking, whether at school or university, at least some of the above scenarios will apply to your studies. You might also notice that there are two kinds of time management in the above situations:

1. 'Micro' time management scenarios such as exams, where you need to manage a short period of time. Usually, you only need to manage your time for a singular task: completing the exam.

2. 'Macro' time management scenarios such as revision season in preparation for your exams. In these situations, you have a much larger amount of time which you need to manage effectively. However, you also probably have a lot more tasks that need completing, so you need to be diligent in your time management.

So, the next chapter will focus on time management in the following areas:

1. Time management in exams.

2. Time management for coursework (such as essays, controlled assessments, and lab work).

3.   Time management for revision.

The next chapter will give you plenty of tips for dealing with the above areas.

Cutting Down on Lost Time

On top of learning how to manage time for revision, coursework, and exams, it helps to learn ways of finding where you're losing time, and how you can get that time back.

Obviously, it's impossible to literally gain back time that you've lost or wasted in the past. However, there are ways to learn from your mistakes, find out where you're losing time, and then plan to get that time back in the future.

Much of this skill comes down to working *smart* as well as working *hard*. While it's admirable to spend days upon days working on an essay plan, it isn't necessarily the amount of time that you spend on something that ensures quality. Rather, it's making effective use of that time to get your work done as efficiently as possible which matters the most. In our chapter on cutting down on lost time, we'll be taking a look at ways in which you can re-think the way you work in order to save time.

A major factor in losing time is procrastination. This most often occurs when you're sitting down to work, but constantly allow yourself to be distracted by the things around you. Avoiding procrastination is key to improving your time management, and so we'll be discussing this in the chapter on cutting down on lost time.

Improving Your Studies

Being able to work hard is incredibly important to academic success, but you need to be able to work *smart* as well. Good time management involves finding ways to make the best use of your time to work efficiently. This involves finding better ways to study for exams, quicker methods of researching for coursework, and ways to improve your speed in an exam scenario to make sure that you have plenty of time to finish the exam. In our chapter on improving your studies, we'll look at methods of working more efficiently in the following three areas:

1.   Exams.

2.   Coursework.

3.   Revision.

You should now have a good idea as to what time management is, where it's useful, and the areas of study that we're going to be looking at in this book to help you improve your time management skills. Let's begin with macro and micro time management.

MICRO AND MACRO TIME MANAGEMENT

In the previous chapter, we mentioned two different kinds of time management that you need to learn and improve in order to excel in your studies. As a reminder, these are:

1. Micro time management: This kind of time management focuses on scenarios with strict time constraints, such as exams.

2. Macro time management: This kind of time management is useful for planning over a longer period of time, such as essay-writing or studying for an exam.

In this chapter, we're going to be looking at tips for both of these areas, giving you the best chance of success in both your exams and the rest of your studies.

Time Management in an Exam - Micro Time Management

When you're in an exam, you have an extremely limited amount of time to complete it. Whether it's 45 minutes or 3 hours, the fact is that you are under strict time constraints. Thankfully, the entirety of this time can be devoted to completing the exam; you don't have to worry about any other tasks or responsibilities while you're in the exam room.

Time management in an exam is pretty straightforward. All you need to do is divide your time in a way which means you have plenty of time to complete every question, to the highest possible standard. There are a few simple ways you can do this.

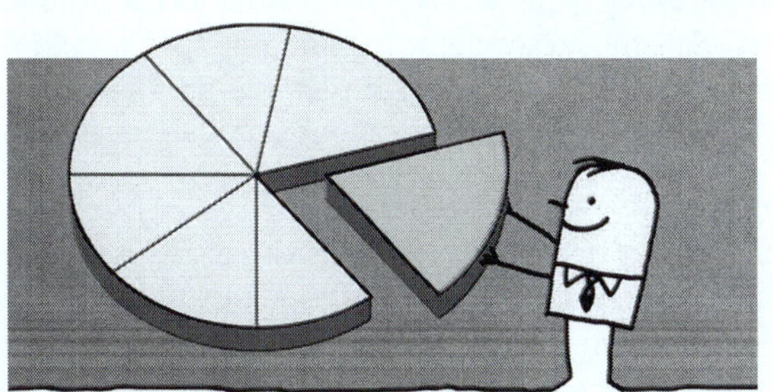

1. Calculate the amount of time you have for each mark.

This is a fairly simple method of figuring out approximately how much time you have in an exam to answer each question. All it takes is a tiny bit of research beforehand, as well as some simple maths which you can do on a calculator. This method is particularly useful for exams in which you have lots of questions to answer, such as Science or Maths papers.

1. Before the exam, find out both the time limit and the total number of marks available. Then, divide the amount of minutes (e.g. 120 minutes) by the total number of available marks (50 marks). This will give you the approximate amount of time you have to secure each mark. In this example, you have 2.4 minutes for each mark.

2. Using this methodology, you can figure out how much time you should spend on each question. In this example, a 1-mark question should be worked on for around 2.4 minutes, a 10-mark question should be attempted for 24 minutes, and so on. If you divide your time like this, you should be able to ensure that you have enough time to answer each question.

3. Remember that these calculations only give you an approximation of how much time you should be spending on a question. Obviously, you're going to need more time to answer questions which you find more difficult, and will probably need less time to attempt questions which you are more comfortable with. This is why it's usually a good idea to take a look through the entire question booklet, scout out every question you'll have to answer, and then quickly figure out how much time you'll need for each question.

2. Divide your time for different essays.

You can use the above method in essay-based exams as well. Let's say that you have two hours to complete an exam (120 minutes). You also have two essay questions to complete. If these are worth the same amount, then you split your time equally so that you have enough time for each. However, if one is worth more than another, you'll need to do some simple maths to figure out how much time you should spend on each.

In this example, let's say you have 120 minutes, and the total available mark is

50. One of the essays is worth a maximum of 30 marks, and the other is worth a maximum of 20 marks. This is a ratio of 3:2. Divide the total amount of time (120) by 5, giving you 24 minutes. This is the amount of time you have to score ten marks. Since one of the essays is worth 30 marks, multiply 24 by 3 to get the amount of time you should spend securing 30 marks (72 minutes). This means that you should spend 72 minutes on the 30-mark question, and the remaining 48 minutes on the 20 mark-question. You can then use these figures to work out how much time you'll need to plan your answer.

3. Create time for planning.

Many students taking essay-based subjects make the mistake of not planning their answers. However, many students *instead* make the mistake of planning an essay, but not taking planning time into account when figuring out how long they have to write their answer. Generally speaking, an essay plan should take somewhere between five and ten minutes, depending on how long the essay is.

The amount of time spent on your plan should be roughly proportional to how much time you have to answer it, and how many marks it's worth. If you only have 15 minutes to write the answer, then there's not much point in spending 5 minutes of it planning! Instead, do a quick 1-2 minute outline of your ideas before getting started.

However, if your essay is going to be much longer, you should take more time to plan. If you have an hour to write your response, you should try to spend 10 minutes on the planning stage. This also gives you an opportunity to remember all of the notes you'll need from all of the revision you've done!

While it's important to devote a good chunk of time to planning your essay, it's just as vital that you don't spend too much time on it. Ultimately, your plan isn't being assessed, so you won't get marked for it! Make sure that you head on to your answer as soon as you've finished planning, and don't waste time.

4. Bring a watch.

In the majority of cases, there will be a large clock at the front of the exam room so that you're able to keep an eye on the time. While this is useful, it requires you to stop and look up fairly frequently to make sure that you have time to write your answers. Rather than stopping to look up at the clock at the front of the room, bring a watch into the exam room so that you can quickly take a look at it without having to stop your train of thought. This way, you'll be able to manage your time more effectively.

5. Wrap it up.

Hopefully, you've given yourself enough time to finish the question with a standard of quality that you're happy with. If this isn't the case, you might find that you're running out of time! If this often happens to you, then you need to learn to cut your losses, wrap up a question as best as you can, and then move on to the next one.

Simply put, there's no great way to abruptly end an essay. However, if you overrun on one answer, your next essay is going to suffer for it. For this reason, you should try and conclude your argument as quickly as possible.

Here are some tips for wrapping up an essay question as quickly as possible so that you can move on to the next one:

1. If you make your essay more focused on a single idea from the very beginning, it's less likely that your answer will get out of hand. If you aren't moving too far away from the main core of your argument, it should be fairly easy to bring it full-circle if you need to finish up quickly.

2. If you're running out of time, finish your essay on the current point that you're making. If possible, try not to shove the rest of your ideas into this paragraph, since this will make your essay look rushed and unsophisticated. Instead, try to link this final point back to the main argument of the essay as best as you can.

3. Don't spend too long on your conclusion. This is generally a good rule when writing essays, but is even more important if you're running out of time. Try to summarise your argument in three sentences or less.

4. Try and save time for some proofreading at the

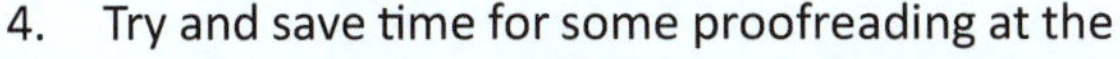

end. However, if you're really short on time, just opt for a quick scan at the end of the test. If you're running out of time, you won't have the opportunity to make any significant changes to your essay anyway. Just try and catch any spelling or grammatical errors on your final read of the essay.

5. If it helps, you can proofread each answer once you've completed it. For example, if you have two essays, then you can start by answering essay one. Once you've finished it, then you can proofread it. After that, move on to essay two. Then, once you've finished that, proofread it at the end. This might prevent you from stressfully reading through multiple essays in the final minutes of the exam.

Of course, not everyone is going to be writing essay questions in their exams. Here's what to do if you're running out of time on your exam and need to move on quickly:

1. Quickly flick through the question paper and find the easiest questions, or the questions you think you can complete as quickly as possible. In the final minutes of your exam, you should just focus on securing as many marks as possible. The best way to do this is to find easier and shorter questions, and complete as many as you can. There's no point getting bogged down on a longer and harder question if you aren't going to be able to get any marks from it.

2. In tests with lots of questions, such as in Maths or Science exams, you should *attempt* as many questions as possible. Some questions will award you for your

working, so you might be able to gain a few marks just for working on the answer.

3. Don't forget to check all of your answers! It might be tempting to write up until the final minute, but this could cost you marks in the event that you've made errors that you didn't spot before.

Whatever kind of exam you're sitting, make sure that you wrap up your answers in as neat a way as possible. Remember to keep your handwriting as neat as possible if you're sitting a handwritten exam!

Time Management for Coursework - Macro Time Management

Time management isn't just important for tense exam situations; it's also extremely useful for when you're completing coursework or doing revision. Here, we're going to take a look at a few things that you can do to improve your time management skills when working on your coursework.

By coursework, we mean any long-form piece of assessed work. This could be a university essay or lab project, or a controlled assessment at school. While these are all very different kinds of task, the following tips apply to all of them.

The major difference between time management during coursework versus exams is the amount of time you have to work with. In an exam, you probably have somewhere between 45 minutes and 3 hours. For coursework, you'll probably have weeks or months to plan, research, and write up your piece.

With the above in mind, coursework has many advantages compared to exams. You have more time to complete it, and therefore you have more freedom in how you spend that time. Of course, the increased amount of time to complete coursework usually reflects the level of quality expected from it. Coursework has to be better researched and planned than an exam, and so you're going to need plenty of time to complete it properly.

Since you're completing coursework over the course of a few weeks or months, you need to be able to balance your time spent on it with your other studies, responsibilities, and your personal life! This can be a challenge in itself, so here we're going to give you some coursework-specific advice for time management:

1. Start early.

This might seem obvious, but many students leave their coursework late before starting it, resulting in a rush towards the end. When you're rushing so much, and worrying about the deadline, you're probably not going to be thinking very rationally about time management. For this reason, we recommend that you at least start planning your coursework long before the deadline, so that you have a good road map of where your work is heading.

2. Plan your hours.

If possible, try to find out from your teacher, lecturer, seminar leader, or tutor about how much time you are expected to devote to the piece of coursework. Hopefully, they'll give a rough number of hours that you're meant to spend on it. Use this as a rough guide for planning out how many hours per week, or per day, that you'll be spending on a piece of work.

So, let's say that you are expected to spend forty hours on a single piece of coursework, and the deadline is in six weeks' time. If you divide forty by six, you'll get 6.66 hours to spend per week on your coursework. This equates to roughly one hour per day. With this in mind, you can decide on how you want to use this time. Some people would divide this time up, giving you one hour per day to work on the coursework. Other students, however, would divide it into two big chunks, maybe working on them on Saturday and Sunday for just under four hours each day. Whatever way you slice it, make sure that you're spending enough time on your coursework. In addition, try to find a plan which works for you. Think about whether you work better in a 1-hour burst per day, or if you need a longer period of time to really dig into your coursework.

3. Remember your other responsibilities!

When planning your coursework, you need to remember everything else you need to do. So, while you might only need to devote 7 hours of time per week to your coursework, you probably have other things to be getting on with as well! Whether it's revision, other pieces of coursework, or your personal life, you need to have created a plan which includes everything else that you're doing. You don't need to plan your entire life down to the second, but it helps to divide each day into hour-long chunks. Then, decide on what you're going to do for that hour: be it coursework, homework, revision, or relaxing.

4. Once you have a plan, stick to it.

A plan is only as good as the discipline behind it. In other words, you need to be prepared to stick to the plan you have made as much as possible. This doesn't mean you need to be completely inflexible - sometimes things crop up that need dealing with, and you can let your studies completely take over your life - but you should attempt to follow your plan as much as you can. This might mean that you need to avoid procrastination more, and need to discipline yourself to knuckle down and work. We'll be taking a look at avoiding procrastination in the next chapter.

5. Remember to take breaks.

Unless you're on a massive roll with your coursework, it's good to take regular breaks so that your mind can recuperate. Generally speaking, our capacity to concentrate starts to wane after about 45 minutes to an hour. So, make sure you take regular short breaks to recharge your concentration. Then, get back into your studying.

While taking breaks is important, make sure you incorporate them into your timetable. Try not to spend too long in your breaks (preferably no longer than 10 minutes), and make sure that you're not taking them too frequently so that you can actually get some work done!

Time Management for Revision - Macro Time Management

On top of exams and coursework, you need to be able to manage your time during revision season. In many ways, this is similar to time management for coursework, but with a few main differences. Here, we'll take a look at how you can manage your time better while revising so that you're always ahead of the game.

1. Find out what you need to revise.

This is an obvious first step, but many students fail to take note of what they need to study before jumping into their revision. By finding out what you need to revise, we mean the following:

1. Find out how many modules you need to cover for each of your exams.

2. Find out exactly what it is you need to know, and separate it from things you *don't* need to know. This will save you a lot of time and effort.

So, begin by getting a list of every module that you need to know about for every exam that you're taking. Then, find out the essentials of every module. If you're studying at school, this can usually be found in the syllabus or curriculum on exam board websites. If you're at university, you might need to go onto your department's website to find out what it is that you need to know.

The reason why you should find out what you *don't* need to know is that you don't want to be wasting time learning material that won't appear in your exam. Try and find out what questions are most likely to show up, and what their general format is. This will help you to organise what you need to know, so you can take note of every topic that needs to be revised.

2. Divide your modules into chunks.

Once you know all of the modules that you'll need to revise, it's time to divide them into chunks to make them easier to manage. Let's take that, for a single exam or subject, you have 16 modules that you need to learn. Rather than seeing this as a huge mass of material, you might find it helpful to divide it into smaller chunks of 2 or 4. So, you go from having a massive 16 modules to 4 chunks, all containing 4 modules. You have the same amount of material to cover, but now you can work at it piece by piece rather than just attacking an overwhelming amount of revision.

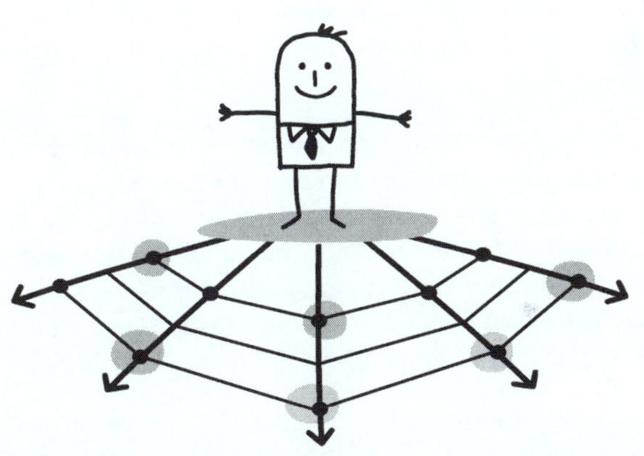

3. Revise through practice.

This method involves bringing the two main aspects of revision together: memorising information and sitting practice papers. When revising for an exam, you need to be knowledgeable about the following areas:

1. The material that you'll need to know in order to answer the questions.

2. The format of the test, and how well you can answer the questions in the time limit.

Practice papers are a great place to improve your skills in both of the above areas, since they test both skills. Let's take a look at how to use practice papers efficiently during your revision.

There are two different ways to use mock exams in your revision. The first way is to attempt a full mock exam as you work through topics of the subject. For example, say that you have a Science exam with three different sections. One of these sections is on evolution and adaptation, the next is on the human anatomy, and the final section is about how drugs and other substances can have an effect on the body. You figure out that these are the three topics you need to learn, so you go through past papers online, focusing on questions revolving around these three topics.

Alternatively, you can work through every topic for the exam, and then move onto past papers. The advantage of this method is that you can spend a chunk of time focusing completely on taking notes and using other revision techniques, then move onto working through whole mock papers. This means that you can simulate the experience of being in an actual exam.

Finding mock exams is usually quite easy. If you're studying at university, the first port of call is your lecturer or seminar tutor, or some other kind of academic advisor. It's possible that they have some mock exams already printed to give to you. If they don't, then it might be worth suggesting that they make some available for yourself and other students.

At most universities, exam papers that students of previous years have taken will be available online or via a local network. Find out where to access them, and get stuck in. However, make sure to check that the module specification has not changed significantly, and that the structure of the exam you will be sitting actually resembles the mock paper! Course tutors and seminar leaders will have all the info you need.

So, while printing pages of past papers can get expensive, it can be a vital way to learn where your strengths lie and where you need to improve. A solution which will allow you to take advantage of mock papers, as well as save you money on printer ink, is to find settings on your printer such as 'draft' or 'ink saver' mode. These will print the past papers out in a slightly lower quality, but usually the papers are still entirely usable.

If you're studying at school, find out what exam board your assessment falls under. Then, head over to their website, where you should be able to find past papers from previous years, as well as sample papers from the beginning of the curriculum.

Once you're finished with the mock paper, look at the mark scheme and see how well you did. For subjects with clear "right or wrong" answers, such as Maths or Science, this is quite easy – all you need to do is read the answer then see if it matches what you wrote. For essay-based subjects such as English, this is trickier since the answers you give aren't necessarily right or wrong. In these exams, you tend to be judged on how well you write rather than what you write exactly. In this case, you might need help from your teacher.

In our final chapter on general time management tips, we'll provide some resources and planning materials for organising your revision, and making use of past papers.

Conclusion

You should now have some ideas for improving your micro and macro time management skills. These tips should get you started on identifying what you're getting right about your time management, as well as where you need to improve. The final chapter of this book will provide even more tips and advice for improving your time management across coursework, revision, and exams. For now, however, we're going to move on to ways of cutting down on lost time.

CUTTING DOWN ON
LOST TIME

As we mentioned earlier, one of the greatest challenges for students who wish to improve their time management skills is how well they stay focused on the task at hand. When you lose focus, you end up losing a little bit of time to procrastination, or simply staring into space. So, in this chapter we'll be taking a look at the following areas:

1.   Staying motivated.

2.   Avoiding procrastination and staying focused.

This is a serious challenge for most students, especially when there's lots of other things they would like to be doing. So, without further ado, let's get started!

How Do I Motivate Myself?

Getting motivated to revise in the first place can be incredibly difficult, and requires a lot of determination and self-control. The earlier you start your revision, the better, but you'll probably be tempted to put off revision: "I'll start next week", or "It's way too early to start revising." Start revising at least six weeks before your first exam. This should give you plenty of time to get through all of your topics.

However, even starting the process can be a pain, and when the exams are so far away it's difficult to get the ball rolling. So, you need to motivate yourself to start revising as early and as well as possible. In this section, we'll take a look at some of the ways you can keep yourself motivated and make sure you get through your revision.

Revision Styles

Start by finding revision styles that you actually enjoy. This might sound ridiculous, but if you can find a few techniques that aren't completely unbearable, you'll be more willing to make a start with revision. Remember that you don't have to be constantly doing 'hard revision' such as note-taking. Mix things up and try a number of styles to keep things fresh early on, then maybe move into something more serious later.

Ease Into It

Before you start, revision can feel like a huge mountain, impossible to climb. It can be incredibly daunting. You might be overwhelmed by the feeling that you are completely unprepared and don't know enough. That said, you need to make a start sometime. Some revision is better than no revision at all, so if you're struggling to get started with your studies, ease your way into it. Start by revising for a much shorter period of time, and maybe focus on the things that you already know well or most enjoy. Once you're comfortable and confident, move onto something that you're less sure of.

Treat Yourself

Make sure you keep yourself motivated with some treats. You don't need to go overboard, but the "carrot and stick" method of revision can keep you working for longer periods of time, allowing you to get through more work. Things like "I'll get some ice cream, but only after I've done the next 3 pages" are a great way of keeping you going and keeping your spirits up.

Think Ahead

Finally, always think ahead past exams. Life continues after your exams. You might feel that you're not in a great place while revising, that your social life is suffering or your free time is being eaten up by studies, but it will all be worth it when you get great results. This positive outlook – thinking towards the future – is one of the best ways to get you started with revision, and keep you going with it too.

Staying Focused

Sometimes, studying can be a total pain, and you'd rather do anything (even sit around doing absolutely nothing!) than open a book and do some hard learning. It's very tempting to procrastinate, but falling into the trap of putting off revision is one of the biggest mistakes you can possibly make.

Here are our top 5 tips for avoiding procrastination and getting on with your work!

Turn Off Distractions

The first thing you should do before starting a revision session is remove any distractions from your workspace. The biggest offenders for distracting students are games consoles, social media, mobile phones, television, and mischievous house-mates. The simple solution to this is to turn off these devices, and put them somewhere out of view or reach, so you aren't tempted to turn them back on and continue texting, messaging or playing games.

Sometimes, however, it isn't practical to move all of these devices. In this case, it's better to find a new workspace, free of electronic devices and other distractions. If there's nowhere in your house or halls that's suitable for studying, the library may be the better choice.

When choosing a place to study, consider the following:

- Is it quiet?

- Are there any gadgets to distract you?

- Will people be walking in and out of the room? Will that distract you?

- Is it comfortable?

- Is there plenty of room for you and all of your notes?

Things get a little trickier when you're using computerised or other online resources such as revision games or podcasts. In these cases, you're going to need your computer, phone or tablet with you, so you'll need to exercise some self-control. Log yourself out of social media if you feel that it's necessary to do so, and make sure to turn off notifications for messaging apps on your phone. You can always take a look during your breaks.

Finally, a few words about listening to music while revising. Be very careful when playing music (especially music with lyrics) while studying. It works for some people, but others will find it incredibly distracting. Experiment with it for yourself, but if you find that it doesn't help you, promptly turn it off.

Give Yourself Plenty of Breaks (but not too many!)
Believe it or not, one of the best ways to avoid procrastination is to take regular breaks. Concentration tends to slide after 45 minutes for a lot of students, so don't push yourself to revise for longer periods of time. If you do this, you'll likely get distracted by almost everything around you, or just get bored or tired. The solution to this problem is to place regular breaks after every chunk of time spent revising.

So, if you revise for 45 minutes, you should give yourself a 10 or 15-minute break afterwards. Start with this and then adjust it as necessary, until you get into a routine which is comfortable for you. Remember not to go overboard with breaks. Make sure that you stick to your timetable and routine, so that a 15-minute break doesn't turn into an hour spent watching TV!

Stick to Your Revision Timetable
Writing and filling in a revision timetable is one thing, but it's another thing entirely to stick to it throughout your entire exam season. If it helps, make your timetable

more detailed to include breaks and other activities.

It can be tempting to put off revision or bargain with yourself: "I'll only do 2 hours today but I'll make up for it tomorrow," or "I don't really need to know this stuff, I'll take the rest of the day off." Both of these are risky mind-sets, which don't put you in a great place for succeeding. Good organisation skills come in handy here, and you should try and keep to your timetable as much as possible.

Of course, you can be flexible with your time. Sometimes things come up, and you shouldn't completely sacrifice your social life during the revision period. Just make sure it's reasonable, though.

Make Your Working Environment Comfortable
Outside of keeping things quiet and free from distracting gadgets, you should make sure that your revision space is comfortable enough for you to work in. If the room is too cold or hot, or your chair isn't comfortable to sit on, then you might find yourself not wanting to revise. Make sure your revision space is as comfortable as possible.

Mix Things Up
The final tip for staying focused is to mix things up every so often. One way to do this,

is to change the subject that you're revising halfway through the day. This means that you'll still be revising, and you'll keep things fresh. You don't need to switch it up too often, but when you find yourself getting too bored of a topic to continue, finish it and then move onto something else entirely, preferably an area from another subject.

You could also change your revision techniques from time to time, to keep things interesting. If you've spent the whole morning writing notes, why not switch over to a podcast or some online resources? You can refer back to our section on different learning styles to get some ideas on how to make your revision more varied.

Cramming (and How to Avoid it!)

Cramming is the act of trying to stuff in as much revision as possible in the days (or even hours!) just before the exam. It's also possibly the biggest act of sabotage that you can do to yourself.

Cramming happens when a candidate either does very little or no revision before the exams. Before they know it, the exam dates have crept up on them, sending them into a state of panic. These candidates tend to then rush through their textbooks and materials, trying to cover weeks' worth of work in just a few days. In almost every case, this is simply not enough time to adequately revise everything. So, people who cram very rarely benefit from it.

Cramming can actually worsen your performance in an exam. Students who cram often find themselves completely blanking on information when they start answering questions, leaving them helpless during an exam. Cramming doesn't work because you aren't giving your brain enough time to let information sink in.

In an ideal world, you should try to finish your revision for a subject 2 or 3 days before the exam starts. This doesn't always go to plan, but aim to have your revision finished at least 2 days before. Revising the night before an exam is a bad idea, and you should avoid doing so. The day before your exam (and in the hours leading up to it as well) should be spent relaxing and keeping calm, eating well and not allowing yourself to become stressed out by looming thoughts about the test. If you get to the day before your exam and you've finished everything, then you've done an excellent job, and deserve an evening to relax.

Creating an Assessment Timetable

Let's assume that you're currently at university, and you've picked your modules for the year. First of all, congratulations – even making it to university is commendable.

From here, you need to start thinking about how you're going to organise your work throughout the year. You've probably got a lot of different modules to study for, and depending on your course this could take all kinds of forms. Prioritising your work and getting ready for the year or term will put you on the right track for achieving a first.

The first thing to do is find out what the assessment structure is for each module that you're taking. Usually, this information can be found on your department website. Take note of how many essays or assignments you have to complete throughout the year, as well as the number of exams you'll be given at the end.

Once you know every piece of work that you have to hand in, you need to find out whether they are assessed as summative work or formative work. Remember, summative assignments count towards your final mark at the end of the year, whilst formative ones do not. For each of the summative assignments, find out how much of the module they are worth. For example, the two essays in a module might make up 40% of the marks in the module overall, whilst the exam is worth 60%. Take note of this, since it will let you figure out what you should prioritise.

With the number and value of each assessment in mind, it's time to get the dates of the deadlines. The exact date might not be made available immediately, but department websites should give a rough indication (for example, 'one essay due at the end of the first term').

Universities and departments will handle these deadlines in different ways. Some courses will have a load of assignments across all of your modules due at around the same time at the end of term, whilst others might stagger them slightly so that you don't feel overwhelmed in the final week of term.

If all of your deadlines land at the same time in the final week of term, don't try to do them all in a short space of time. Try to find out the assignment task as early as possible during the term so that you can get started on them as soon as possible.

Take a look at the following table, which suggests how you might want to approach assignments during the year. This table assumes that each essay takes one week to complete. Depending on the amount of preparation you need to do for each, and how fast you are at working, this might take more time. Also, bear in mind that you might have more assessments than this, or potentially less.

Week	Essays	Deadlines
1		
2		
3		
4	Essay 1	
5	Essay 2	
6	Essay 3	
7	Essay 4	Essay 1
8	Essay 5	
9	Essay 6	Essay 2, Essay 3
10		Essay 4, Essay 5, Essay 6

Here, you can see how each essay is completed well before its deadline. Completing Essay 1 in Week 4 means that it's finished with two weeks spare. This means that, if you need to go back and make some final adjustments, there's plenty of time to do so. This method of spacing out your assessments means that you aren't overworking yourself at the end of term. Make an assignment plan so that each piece of assessed work gets enough attention.

Next, you need to consider which assessments should take priority. Of course, you should try to complete everything to an equal standard. Even if an assessment is formative, submitting it with as much effort put into it as possible will still be helpful for the following reasons:

1. Formative assessments can be used to consolidate your own knowledge on areas you might need for summative assessments or exams later in the year.

2. They're a great form of practice, especially for essay-based modules.

3. You'll likely receive feedback from the person who marked your work, letting you know whether you're on the right track or not.

For these reasons, you should take formative assessments seriously. However, sometimes you'll be faced with a lot of summative work that simply needs to take precedence. If you have to, prioritise the work that directly affects your overall grade at the end of the year. However, this doesn't mean you should ignore formative work

– it's also extremely important.

Creating a Revision Timetable

The goal of having a revision timetable is to map out all of the work that needs to be done in time for each exam. Your plan doesn't need to be expertly crafted or even particularly nice to look at, it just needs to be clear and easy to read.

The first thing you should do is list every subject that you are taking exams in. Once you've done that, try and find every topic or module within that subject. For example, a breakdown of AS level Biology may look like this:

1.   **Molecules**

- Polymers;

- Carbohydrates;

- Lipids;

- Proteins;

- DNA.

2. **Cells**

- The structure of cells;

- The structure of viruses;

- Cell membranes;

- The immune system.

3. **Organisms and their environment**

- Surface area to volume ratio;

- Gas exchange;

- Digestion;

- Mass transport.

4. **Genetic information**

- DNA, genes and chromosomes;

- Protein synthesis;

- Genetic diversity;

- Taxonomy and Species;

- Biodiversity.

You may wish to go into slightly more detail for each of the topics, but as a foundation, this will be enough to fill in a revision timetable. Do this for every module and for every subject, so that you know roughly how much material there is to cover. It's also worth taking a look at how long each of the chapters for these modules are in your textbook, so that you're aware of any abnormally large or small topics.

Once you've done this, it's time to prioritise all of your subjects and topics. Some people like to rank all their subjects from most important to least important. In other words, it might be worth considering which subjects you find more difficult, and giving them higher priority. If you already feel quite confident about a certain part of your studies, place it slightly lower on your list. This means that the areas that need the most attention will receive it.

Once you've prioritised your subjects, you can also prioritise modules. Bear in mind that a lot of topics in many subjects are cumulative – which means that a good understanding of earlier modules is vital for getting to grips with later ones. This is especially the case with Maths and Science, where you're building up knowledge as you go along. For these ones, it's better to start at the beginning and work your way

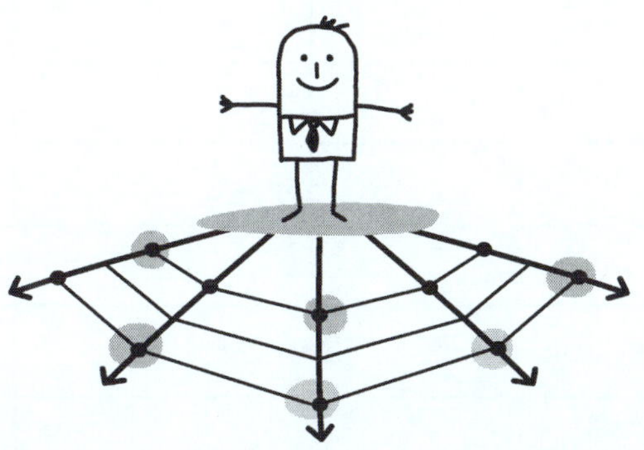

Your timetable should include all of the material that you need to revise outside of school hours. The best way to find out what you need to cover, is to take a look at how your textbooks divide their content, and then use those to fill the timetable. You'll be treated to some blank templates for a timetable at the end of this book.

The following example timetable shows what a single week of revision may look like. Take a look at this timetable to get an idea of how to organise your time.

	Monday	Tuesday	Wednesday
09:00 - 10:00	School	School	School
10:00 - 11:00	School	School	School
11:00 - 12:00	School	School	School
12:00 - 13:00	School	School	School
13:00 - 14:00	School	School	School
14:00 - 15:00	School	School	School
15:00 - 16:00	Break	Break	Break
16:00 - 17:00	Biology - Polymers	Biology - Proteins	Biology - Cell Structure
17:00 - 18:00	Biology - Carbohydrates	Biology - DNA	Biology - Virus Structure
18:00 - 19:00	Biology - Lipids	English Lit - Reading Poetry	English Lit - Revising Quotes

Thursday	Friday	Saturday	Sunday
School	School	Biology - Digestion	Biology - Mock Exam
School	School	Biology - Mass Transport	Biology - Mark Scheme
School	School	Biology - DNA	Biology - Free Revision
School	School	Break	Break
School	School	Biology - Genetic Diversity	Biology - Free Revision
School	School	Biology - Taxonomy and Species	Biology - Free Revision
Break	Break	Break	Break
Biology - Cell Membranes	Biology - Surface to Volume Ratio	Biology - Biodiversity	English Lit - Free Revision
Biology - The Immune System	Biology - Gas Exchange	English Lit - Reading Poetry	English Lit - Free Revision
English Lit - Reading Shakespeare	English Lit - Revising Quotes	English Lit - Reading Shakespeare	English Lit - Free Revision

Using Checklists

A great way to cut down on lost time when working on a project is to create a checklist of everything that needs doing, and then sticking to it as closely as possible. This way, you can ensure that you're only dedicating your time to things you *need* to do.

In order to create an effective checklist, you'll need the following:

1. A list of tasks that you need to complete. This can be a list of modules you need to know for an exam, a list of past papers that need completing, or a number of tasks that you need to complete for a project such as an essay.

2. An approximate amount of time necessary to complete **everything** that you need to complete.

Once you have these, you'll be ready to make your checklist. We'll provide some blank checklists at the end of this book.

Creating Your Checklist

Once you have a list of tasks and areas to focus on, you should take another look at them to find out the following:

- What sub-tasks need completing? For example, one of your tasks may be to "research for an essay". This might involve visiting the library to get some books, taking a look at some online databases, or doing lab work in order to gather data. These will need to be considered in your checklist as well as the overall task of "research an essay".

- What other tasks need doing? These can be unrelated to the actual subject, but are things you also need to do that day. For example, this could be 'go shopping for food'. While it isn't necessary to complete the task, it's something you'll need to do that day. Therefore, you should include it in your checklist.

- What tasks *don't* need doing? This might seem odd, but it's a good idea to remove any tasks which you don't need to do that day, that week, or at all. For revision at university, it might be the case that you only need to pick a selection of modules and topics for an exam, since you'll be given a choice of essay questions in the real test. If this applies to you, then make sure that your checklist does not include irrelevant and unnecessary tasks which could result in you losing time.

- Prioritise your tasks in order of importance, or place them in chronological order. Make sure the process makes sense, so you can tick tasks off as you go. Research for an essay should usually happen before or during the planning stage, not after it. Therefore, make sure 'research the essay' is written before 'plan the essay'. If there is no strict chronological order for your tasks, then place them in order of importance. Therefore, you'll be forcing yourself to deal with the crucial tasks before moving onto less important ones. This will greatly aid your productivity as you methodically move through your work.

Using Your Checklist

Once you've created your checklist, you need to start making use of it! If it's hand-written or you've printed it out, place your checklist somewhere that's easy to see and that you'll be looking at often, such as on the wall near where you do your studying. If you've got your checklist on your computer or phone, make sure that it's easily accessible, such as placing a shortcut on the desktop of your computer or the 'home' screen of your phone.

Once you've got your checklist in a good location, it's time to start on your work. As you work through your checklist, tick off the tasks that you've completed. Leave space for notes on your checklist if possible, so that you can include any details that you might need to remember later. Finally, try and give a time and date of completion on each task, so that you can look back and have a good idea about how long each task took. This way, you can plan for future assignments by using previous timings as general guidance for how long a piece of work takes you to complete. This will help you to tighten up your timings, so that you can cut down on lost time as you work through your assignments.

Conclusion

In this chapter, we've taken a look at a few ways you can cut down on lost time by cutting out the biggest threat to productivity: procrastination. In addition, we've also discussed ways of cutting down on lost time by planning your assessments and revision schedules, as well as using checklists to keep track of how far through you are with your work. In the next chapter, we'll be taking a look at some ways in which you can make the most out of your studies to make you even more efficient with your time!

IMPROVING YOUR STUDIES

One of the most important parts of time management is being able to make effective use of the time you have. After all, you can save all of the time in the world, but if the quality isn't there then you haven't made effective use of that time. In this chapter, we'll be looking at some time-efficient ways of dealing with exams, revision, and coursework.

Exam Tips

When it comes to exams, it's all about two things: speed and quality. You need to work as best as you can, in a short space of time. Before we begin to look at general tips for exams, remember the following:

While you need to work quickly during an exam, it is by no means a race to the finish line. In most exams, you won't receive anything for finishing much earlier. In fact, finishing much earlier than the time limit usually means that you've done something wrong! Use every second you have to read the questions, write your answers, and then proofread them.

Now, let's take a look at some top tips for acing your exams, and in turn improving the quality of your work in a shorter time frame.

Practise Handwriting Beforehand

If your exams are handwritten, you need to make sure that your handwriting is legible. In the exam room, people tend to write incredibly quickly. As the exam goes on, some students will write more frantically, while others might slowly ease into the exam and get better as time goes on. Either way, ensure that your handwriting is easy to read.

It might be tempting to write as quickly as humanly possible, since it seems that it will save you time. If the examiner can't read what you've written, they won't be able to mark your work. Generally speaking, it's only the most severe handwriting that results in a significant loss of marks, but if you know that your handwriting isn't as good as it could be, it's worth taking some time to practise it. You don't want to have to waste time during your exam re-writing content so that it's legible.

If possible, try to incorporate handwriting practice into your revision so that you save time. Dedicated handwriting time is good, but you may as well kill two birds with one stone and use revision techniques that help your handwriting, such as making flashcards or writing out pages of notes. If you've been doing mock papers under timed conditions, this should have helped as well.

In the exam, make sure to take your time if you feel as though your handwriting is suffering. If it helps, ditch cursive (joined-up) handwriting so that the words are easier to read.

Finally, you want to practise handwriting so that your muscles are used to writing for extended periods of time. This is important for avoiding hand cramp. Find a way of gripping the pen which is as comfortable as possible, whilst also being able to write efficiently and neatly. Learning some exercises to gently warm up your hands before the exam can also be helpful, and will hopefully make you less worried about your hands giving up halfway through.

If your assessments are based on the computer, you obviously don't need to worry about handwriting. However, if you need to type out your answers, take some time to work on your typing so that you can answer questions quickly and with no typing errors. Being able to touch-type is preferable, but not necessary – just make sure that you can type at a decent pace and with a high level of accuracy.

Keep Calm

Getting a handle on your nerves can be really difficult during exam season, but remember that this is completely normal. If you consider that doing well in your exams is very important, then it would be bizarre for you not to be at least a bit nervous. Millions of people will be going through the same thing as you, and millions more have been in your position and have made it out of the other end in one piece. Life goes on after your exam, even if it doesn't feel like that during the heat of the moment.

Exams are stressful, and the conditions you take them in aren't pleasant either. Being stuck in a silent room for an hour, with nothing but a question paper and your own thoughts, can be incredibly daunting. However, you need to remember that you're not the only one who feels this way, and that a bit of nerves can give you the boost you need in the exam hall.

That being said, you need to keep any anxiety under control. A breakdown just before the exam (or even worse, during it) is uncommon, but just remember that not doing as well as you'd hoped in a single exam isn't the end of the world.

You might feel as though you aren't prepared enough, or perhaps a fellow student has made you unsure about what you've revised – minutes before entering the exam room. This happens often, and can be incredibly demoralising. Remember that how prepared you think you are doesn't necessarily represent how well prepared you actually are. Sometimes, people who feel poorly prepared for some exams in the minutes before taking it end up doing incredibly well, and some people find themselves doing worse in exams that they felt completely ready for. Essentially, you never truly know how prepared you are.

Besides, what's the use in worrying on the day of the exam? There's no time left to go back and revise some more, so there's no point in getting stressed about it once you're in the room. Try and get into the current moment and power through it.

Here are some other tips for keeping calm in the exam:

1. Breathing exercises. If you find yourself getting nervous before exams, or struggle to get to sleep due to exam anxiety, then breathing exercises could be beneficial.

2. Get into the moment. Just before and during your exam, it can help to go into "exam-mode". By this, we mean blocking off outside distractions and any negativity coming from anywhere. Sometimes, having friends and classmates talk about the possible contents of the exam just before entering can put you off. It might make you feel as if you've missed out on something major, and then cause you to worry once you enter the exam room. Put all of this out of your mind as soon as you enter the room. Once you're in the exam, there's no use fretting about those details.

3. Positive thinking. This might seem obvious, but thinking positively about the exam and what comes after can be extremely helpful. Some people like to

change their mind-set about exams, thinking of it as an opportunity to show off their knowledge, rather than as a painful task that they have to work their way through. Alternatively, focus on what you do know rather than what you don't know, what you can do rather than what you can't do. Once you're in the exam room, there's no point worrying about your weaknesses. Focus on your strengths.

If you do find yourself having to stop for a few minutes to calm yourself, don't become stressed by the idea that you're wasting time. It's better to spend a smaller amount of time on your exam if it means you'll be in a better state of mind to tackle it properly, than to rush through it in a panic. Take your time to relax before diving into the exam.

Read Instructions Carefully

This sounds simple, but far too many people trip up on this simple bit of advice. When you enter your exam, the first thing you should do is read the instructions on the front of the question or answer paper. In some cases, an invigilator may read the instructions to you, but feel free to read the instructions before the exam starts.

Keep an eye out for instructions on what questions to answer. In some exams, you'll have a choice, rather than having to answer every question. In these cases, you need to make sure that you know exactly what's required of you, so that you don't waste time answering questions that you don't need to answer. The only thing worse than finding out at the end of the exam that you answered questions unnecessarily, is realising that you didn't answer enough of them!

When you are given a choice of two or more questions to answer (especially in essay subjects), make sure you clearly show which questions you are answering. In some exams, you'll have to tick a box to show what question you're attempting, whilst others will require you to write the question number in your answer section. Either way, keep an eye on the instructions before going ahead and starting the question. This will prevent you from wasting time answering questions that you don't need to attempt, and also stop you from accidentally missing questions that need answering.

Answer the Easiest Questions First
This tip is absolutely key for the tougher exams you come across, since it's an excellent way to use your time in the exam hall effectively.

Say you're about to sit an exam. You sit down and have the examination instructions read out to you. The invigilator instructs you to start your exam, and then you begin. You open the question booklet to find that the first question seems almost impossible. Before you panic, take a flick through the booklet and take a look at some of the other questions. If possible, pick the question that looks the easiest to you and start with that.

This is a good technique for two reasons. Firstly, it's a great boost to your confidence when you're feeling unsure about the exam. There's not much worse in an exam than sitting there, becoming more and more demoralised by a question that you don't think you can answer. Starting with more manageable questions will help you ease into the exam, and hopefully you'll recall some information while doing it.

Sometimes, exams can fit together like a puzzle. At first, it seems impossible. But, once you start to put pieces in (answer the questions), the more difficult bits start to make sense. All of a sudden, you're on a roll of answering questions, and then the tough ones don't seem so bad!

The other reason that this is a good technique, is that it represents a good use of your time. There's no point sitting and staring blankly at a question that you can't solve, when there are others that you could be getting on with. Forget about the tough questions for now, bank as many marks you can get with the easier ones, then go back to the hard ones at the end if you have time. This way, you can secure as many marks as possible. In the worst-case scenario, you won't be able to complete the tough questions, but you'll still have earned a few points for all of the others.

Answer the Question

One of the biggest mistakes that students make throughout their academic lives is failing to answer the question that they've actually been asked. This is particularly the case for essay-based exams such as English Literature, but applies to all of your exams.

Focus on Key Details

Some students have a tendency to read a question briefly, then jump straight into their answer without thinking about what's really being asked. For questions which are worth lots of marks, you should take extra care in reading the question fully. If it helps, underline the key parts of the question, so that it's easier to break down:

What were the main causes of the First World War?

This becomes:

What were the <u>main causes</u> of the <u>First World War</u>?

We can figure out a few things from underlining the key points in this question. Firstly, we know that the topic of the question is the First World War. In particular, we need to be looking at the causes of the war. So, our answer is going to be focused on the time period leading up to the start of the First World War in 1914.

However, there's more to the question than this. This question specifies the "main" causes of the First World War. So, we don't need to talk about every single cause of the war, just a few of the most important or biggest things which caused the First World War to happen, such as the assassination of Archduke Franz Ferdinand and rising tensions between the European empires.

Already, we've figured out that we need to answer the question in the following way:

- You need to talk about the causes of the First World War (events up to 1914);

- You need to limit your answer to the main (biggest) causes of the war.

Highlighting the key points of the question has proven useful, because it's pointed out exactly what the question is asking of us. This means that we can save time by answering exactly what we need to, rather than talking about things that won't get us any extra marks.

Don't Twist the Question

Sometimes, students see a question that they don't particularly like the look of. Perhaps it's for a topic that they've studied well and enjoyed, but the question takes a slightly different direction to one that they're used to. For example, a student may have studied the Shakespeare play Othello as part of English Literature, and really liked the dastardly villain, Iago. In the exam, they might come across a question on the play, but not specifically about Iago. The question could be:

> **How does Shakespeare show the relationship between Othello and his wife, Desdemona?**

This question is primarily focused on the main character, Othello, and his wife, Desdemona. While the character of Iago plays into most elements of Othello, it might be tricky to include him in a discussion about the relationship between Othello and Desdemona. So, you'd need to avoid straying from the topic of the question, even if there's something you would rather write about. Twisting the question into something that you want to answer is a trap that quite a lot of students fall into, and this ends up costing them marks – particularly in essay subjects. Writing a short plan for your answer, and reading the question carefully, can help you avoid this.

Double-Check the Question

We've talked about proofreading your answers, but it's just as important to double-check the question that you're answering, before you begin to answer it.

Say you're doing a maths question:

$$8.93 \times 9.54 = ?$$

Before you start answering the question, take note of everything about it. Where are the decimal points? What operation needs to be performed? Sometimes, people make silly mistakes and misread the question, getting things mixed up.

It's not pleasant finding out that you've answered a question incorrectly just as you get to the end of it, so it pays to look over the question multiple times. In the case of maths questions, it might help to re-write the question in the answer box if there's space. This means you can look back at it quickly, without making any mistakes.

Don't Hedge Your Bets

Hedging your bets happens when a student tries to give 2 or more answers to a single question, trying to cover as many bases as possible and be less likely to lose marks. After all, if you give lots of different answers, surely one of them is bound to be correct? The problem with this is that examiners will mark harshly against answers like these. Take a look at this example of someone who has tried to hedge their bets:

Question: What part of the human body carries blood back to the heart?

Answer: Veins/Arteries

Only one of the given answers can be correct, since one of them sends blood away from the heart and the other brings blood back to it. The correct answer is "veins", but in this example, both possible answers have been put in. This example answer shows that whoever answered the question wasn't sure, so put both down just in case. You can fall into the same trap in longer or even essay responses. Examiners will not award marks for this, so it's essential that you don't try to play it safe in this way. Be confident in your answer.

Revision Tips

Along with ways to improve your time management in exams, we've included some ways to make your revision more time efficient. This includes making use of practice papers, mark schemes, and examiners' reports to make the most of your time when revising.

Simulating Exam Conditions with Practice Papers

Mock papers and past papers are really useful because they allow you to sit a test as if it was the real thing. To do this, find out how much time you would be given to finish the paper in an actual exam – this information can usually be found on the front of the past paper. Then, gather your pens, pencils and other tools, put your notes aside and find a quiet place. Then, get to work with the mock test.

Time yourself with a clock or stopwatch (most mobile phones come equipped with a stopwatch), and see how long it takes you to complete the paper. What's even more useful is to time how long each section, or even each question, takes you to complete. So, if you find yourself running short on time, you know exactly which topics or types of question need greater focus. You don't want to try and speed through your paper too quickly, but if you're taking an unusually long amount of time on shorter questions, then you know that you need to improve on them.

The best part of using mock exams and past papers is that you can put yourself to the test, and make sure of two things. Firstly, you can make sure that you can recall the material you'll need to remember in the real exam. This comes into effect when you simulate a real exam environment, by doing the test under timed conditions and without your notes. While you're doing the mock tests, you'll probably get an idea of what you can and can't recall. Whenever you can't remember the answer to a question, or there's a key fact you can't recall, make a note on a spare sheet of paper, or at the side of your answer booklet. Then, once you finish the paper, you know exactly what you need to go back to and revise some more.

Mock tests are also useful because they highlight things that you thought you knew, but perhaps didn't get entirely correct. Take a look at the following sections on mark schemes.

Mark Schemes

Once you've done some practice papers, you'll want to know how well you've done. As we've mentioned previously, mock papers show you what you need to remember, what you know and what you need to improve on. However, sitting the paper is only half of the story. You'll also need to use a mark scheme to figure out what you do and don't know.

What are Mark Schemes?

Mark schemes are papers which examiners use when marking your exam. In the case of past papers, the mark schemes are the same ones which official A-Level examiners would use to mark your exams. So, they're the most accurate source for answers. Depending on the exam, a mark scheme will include different content. For example, Science exams will often simply give the correct answers since the questions are either right or wrong.

However, answers to essays in English papers aren't as straightforward. For exams with plenty of essay questions, the examiner will have criteria that they will need to look for in order to figure out what the quality of your work is. This is reflected in the mark scheme with a detailed description of what a higher-level essay will look like, and will compare it to other essays of all quality levels. This can make it difficult to mark your own essays, so having your teacher mark them is very useful.

Mark schemes and answer sections can usually be found in the same place where you downloaded the practice papers. Keep away from looking at the mark schemes until you've finished the papers – you don't want to spoil the tests – but have them ready to go.

What are the Benefits of Using Mark Schemes?

Exam Criteria – Essays

Mark schemes have uses beyond simply finding out whether you have got the answers right or wrong. In fact, reading mark schemes can be useful even if you aren't sitting a past paper because they'll show you what type of answers that the examiners are looking for. This is especially the case in essay-based exams, such as English, as well as other exams which include essays, such as Modern Foreign Languages, History and Geography. You can use mark schemes to find out what criteria the examiners use to mark your exams, and then compare what you've written to see how well you've done. Have you mentioned the key information that's listed for each answer? Have you answered the questions clearly, using an appropriate structure? Have you checked your spelling? All of these are going to be picked up on in essay-based exams, but it's worth reading a mark scheme to see how much each of these aspects affect your grade.

Jumping Through Hoops and Keywords

The other useful aspect of mark schemes is that they'll reveal key phrases and terms. A-Level is slightly different to GCSEs in this regard. At GCSE, you're often being tested on sheer knowledge and your ability to recall information. This means that knowing the key words is extremely important at GCSE level, and you can often net marks simply by dropping the key words into your answer.

However, this changes at A-Level. While knowing key terms is still important, in many subjects you're being assessed on understanding rather than regurgitation of key facts. This means that, while key terms are important, you won't automatically earn marks just by mentioning them. Quite often, they have to have some kind of explanation, or application to a scenario. You'll need to engage your brain more for A-Levels.

With all this said, knowing what key terms tend to secure the marks is important for succeeding in certain subjects at A-Level. You will need to remember key words in order to get better marks.

Exact Breakdown of Marks

Mark schemes can also be used to get an exact breakdown of an answer. Using the same example, the answer may award a single mark for lots of different things. For example, a question in a Biology paper could look like the following:

How does an asthma attack reduce airflow?

One answer given could be:

When an asthma attack occurs, airflow is reduced because the following three things happen. Firstly, the muscle walls of the bronchioles tighten and contract, leading to a narrower space. Secondly, more mucus is produced by the bronchioles. Combined, this results in the diameter of the airways decreasing in size. This results in airflow being reduced.

For this example, let's assume two things. Firstly, let's accept this as an entirely correct answer – it got full marks. Also, let's say that this answer is worth three marks. The mark scheme may distribute the marks as follows:

> 1 mark for mentioning each of the following:
>
> - *Muscle walls of bronchioles contract/tighten;*
>
> - *The bronchioles produce more mucus;*
>
> - *Diameter of the airways are reduced.*

Now that we know what got us the marks, we can highlight them in the answer.

When an asthma attack occurs, airflow is reduced because the following three things happen. Firstly, the <u>muscle walls of the bronchioles tighten and contract</u>, leading to a narrower space. Secondly, <u>more mucus is produced by the bronchioles</u>. Combined, this results in the <u>diameter of the airways decreasing in size</u>. This results in airflow being reduced.

So, the breakdown of marks tells you exactly what you need to include in your answer, which will give you an idea of what you need to remember for the exam. Bear in mind that you might need to know more than what's given in the mark schemes, since you could be faced with a question which tackles the same topic but from a slightly different angle.

This information in the mark scheme means you could focus your answer even more. You might notice that a lot of the example answer is not underlined, and these details might not be necessary in order to gain full marks. With the information in the mark scheme, we can simplify and focus our answer:

> Firstly, the muscle walls of the bronchioles contract. More mucus is produced by the bronchioles. Both of these reduce the diameter of the airways. This results in reduction in airflow.

Now this answer is much shorter, but should earn you the same amount of marks. So, we now have a much shorter answer, which will give us as many marks as the longer answer would. This saves time, allowing us to move onto other questions in the exam.

'Waffling' is what people tend to do when they aren't sure how to answer a question. Students who waffle in an exam will add lots of extra words to their answers to fill them out, even if none of what they are saying will earn them marks. Reading a mark scheme and finding out exactly what earns you points should help you to avoid writing meaningless rubbish!

Giving Precise Answers

In an exam, you might be tempted to fire off everything you know about a topic all at once. While it's great that you've remembered lots of information, it's not always a good idea to write absolutely everything you know when answering a question. Instead, you should figure out exactly what the question is asking from you. In the first example, we included a lot of information that wasn't necessary to get full marks.

You should aim to be as precise as possible with your answer – get straight to the point in order to save time. Mark schemes are useful here, because they'll show you what the examiners are looking for. You can figure out what's required to get full marks in a question, then focus on giving that as your answer. In an exam, every second is precious; the less time you spend on unnecessary information, the more time you have for harder questions or for double-checking your work at the end. Efficiency is a great skill to have when it comes to exams, and using mark schemes to hone your answers will help you to achieve this.

Coursework Tips

Alongside revision and exams, you need some ways of honing your coursework skills so that you can make efficient use of your time. Let's take a look at some ways in which you can be time-efficient while doing your coursework.

Start as Soon as Possible

Many students make the mistake of putting coursework off because they think the deadline is far off in the distance. You might not need to write up the final piece until months away, so why bother doing any work now? This is an easy trap to fall into, but must be avoided to perform well. Find out from your teacher as soon as possible what the topic of your coursework is, and what suitable work you can do. In some cases, this might be reading or research, whilst in other scenarios it could be simply becoming familiar with the material. Whatever the case, try to get started as soon as you can – it'll pay off as you approach the deadline.

Make use of Multiple Drafts

If you are doing a long-term piece of coursework that allows for the teacher to read and mark your work, make use of it. Some students will simply work on their draft, finish it and then forget about their coursework until the deadline, when they hand in the exact same piece of work. Multiple drafts are there to help you refine your work, so make use of them as much as possible.

Listen to Feedback

If you get the opportunity to have your drafts read by a teacher, listen and take on board what they suggest you improve on. Sometimes it can be difficult to look at criticism of your work, but it's essential if you want to make your coursework better. Bear in mind that your teacher is there to help you, not attack your work or embarrass you.

Don't Try to Finish it in one Sitting

Some students try to complete all of their coursework in one go – usually the night before the deadline. This is never a good idea, and often results in rushed work full of errors. On page 46, we provided an example week-by-week plan of how to bring a piece of coursework to completion. Create one of these for yourself and follow it to make sure that you aren't suddenly faced with a mountain of work the night before the deadline.

Proofread

Proofreading has been talked about in the exam techniques section, but it's just as important when completing coursework. Double check everything you've written or made. If possible, compare it to a mark scheme, to ensure that you have met all of the requirements to get the grade that you want.

Depending on what kind of coursework you're doing, you're going to want to look out for different things. Of course, checking spelling, punctuation and grammar is important for any piece of work, but you also need to make sure that the content is sound as well. If you've included statistics or other facts in your work, go and compare what you've written to the place you found the information. Do the numbers all add up? Are the facts correct? Make sure that what you've presented is as accurate as possible before submission.

Avoid Plagiarism

Plagiarism is the act of reproducing somebody else's work without their permission, and is taken very seriously by both schools and exam boards – especially when it comes to coursework. It isn't so much of a concern in exams, since copying someone else's work is difficult and doesn't happen often, but in coursework there are lots of regulations to make sure that students hand in work that is their own. This could be one of the reasons why coursework has moved from a less-restricted, open task, to something more structured and controlled, with students finishing their controlled assessment in a classroom while being supervised.

Whatever the case, avoiding plagiarism is vital when completing coursework. Not only is it against regulations and can result in your work being disqualified, but it's also unfair on the people who have worked hard to create the material that you might be copying. Whether it's your classmate, a website, or a book, you should never copy someone else's work.

CONCLUSION

You've now reached the end of *Rapid Skills for Students: Ace Your Time Management.* By using this book, you've given yourself the skills to plan your time more effectively, whether you're revising for tests, sitting exams, or completing coursework and controlled assessments. Bear the information in this book in mind whilst planning your work.

A Few Final Words...

For any test, it is helpful to keep the following in mind...

The Three 'P's

1. Preparation. Preparation is key to passing any test or essay; you won't be doing yourself any favours by not taking the time to prepare. Many fail at university because they did not know what to expect or did not know what their own weaknesses were. Take the time to go over any areas you may have struggled with. By doing this, you will become familiar with how you will perform when it comes to writing your essay.

2. Perseverance. If you set your sights on a goal and stick to it, you are more likely to succeed. Obstacles and setbacks are common when trying to achieve something great, and you shouldn't shy away from them. Instead, face the tougher parts of your course even if you feel defeated. If you need to, take a break from your work to relax and then return with renewed vigour. If you fail the test or essay, take the time to consider why you failed, gather your strength and try again.

3. Performance. How well you perform will be the result of your preparation and perseverance. Remember to relax when taking the test and try not to panic. Believe in your own abilities, practise as much as you can, and motivate yourself constantly. Nothing is gained without hard work and determination, and this applies to your university course as much as anything else in life.

We wish you the best of luck in all of your future endeavours!

USEFUL RESOURCES

	Monday	Tuesday	Wednesday
09:00 - 10:00			
10:00 - 11:00			
11:00 - 12:00			
12:00 - 13:00			
13:00 - 14:00			
14:00 - 15:00			
15:00 - 16:00			
16:00 - 17:00			
17:00 - 18:00			
18:00 - 19:00			

Thursday	Friday	Saturday	Sunday

	Monday	Tuesday	Wednesday
09:00 - 10:00			
10:00 - 11:00			
11:00 - 12:00			
12:00 - 13:00			
13:00 - 14:00			
14:00 - 15:00			
15:00 - 16:00			
16:00 - 17:00			
17:00 - 18:00			
18:00 - 19:00			

Thursday	Friday	Saturday	Sunday

	Monday	Tuesday	Wednesday
09:00 - 10:00			
10:00 - 11:00			
11:00 - 12:00			
12:00 - 13:00			
13:00 - 14:00			
14:00 - 15:00			
15:00 - 16:00			
16:00 - 17:00			
17:00 - 18:00			
18:00 - 19:00			

Thursday	Friday	Saturday	Sunday

	Monday	Tuesday	Wednesday
09:00 - 10:00			
10:00 - 11:00			
11:00 - 12:00			
12:00 - 13:00			
13:00 - 14:00			
14:00 - 15:00			
15:00 - 16:00			
16:00 - 17:00			
17:00 - 18:00			
18:00 - 19:00			

Thursday	Friday	Saturday	Sunday

	Monday	Tuesday	Wednesday
09:00 - 10:00			
10:00 - 11:00			
11:00 - 12:00			
12:00 - 13:00			
13:00 - 14:00			
14:00 - 15:00			
15:00 - 16:00			
16:00 - 17:00			
17:00 - 18:00			
18:00 - 19:00			

Thursday	Friday	Saturday	Sunday

	Monday	Tuesday	Wednesday
09:00 - 10:00			
10:00 - 11:00			
11:00 - 12:00			
12:00 - 13:00			
13:00 - 14:00			
14:00 - 15:00			
15:00 - 16:00			
16:00 - 17:00			
17:00 - 18:00			
18:00 - 19:00			

Thursday	Friday	Saturday	Sunday

	Monday	Tuesday	Wednesday
09:00 - 10:00			
10:00 - 11:00			
11:00 - 12:00			
12:00 - 13:00			
13:00 - 14:00			
14:00 - 15:00			
15:00 - 16:00			
16:00 - 17:00			
17:00 - 18:00			
18:00 - 19:00			

Thursday	Friday	Saturday	Sunday

	Monday	Tuesday	Wednesday
09:00 - 10:00			
10:00 - 11:00			
11:00 - 12:00			
12:00 - 13:00			
13:00 - 14:00			
14:00 - 15:00			
15:00 - 16:00			
16:00 - 17:00			
17:00 - 18:00			
18:00 - 19:00			

Thursday	Friday	Saturday	Sunday

Task Number	Completed?	Time of Completion	Notes

Task Number	Completed?	Time of Completion	Notes

Task Number	Completed?	Time of Completion	Notes

Task Number	Completed?	Time of Completion	Notes

Task Number	Completed?	Time of Completion	Notes

Task Number	Completed?	Time of Completion	Notes

Task Number	Completed?	Time of Completion	Notes

Task Number	Completed?	Time of Completion	Notes

Task Number	Completed?	Time of Completion	Notes

Task Number	Completed?	Time of Completion	Notes

Get Access To

FREE

Psychometric

Tests

www.PsychometricTestsOnline.co.uk

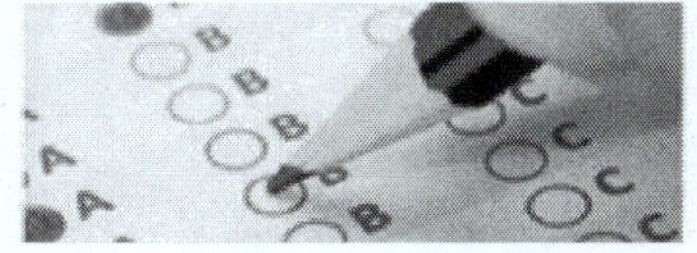

Printed and bound by CPI Group (UK) Ltd, Croydon, CR0 4YY

06/07/2026

02157570-0005